Rhapsody in Retrograde

Lyrical Loops In Verse
Indi Riverflow

Amana Mission Publishing Ink
Alternative Press

To Incite Insight

www.amanamission.com

Rhapsody In Retrograde:
Lyrical Loops In Verse
Indi Riverflow

ISBN-13: 978-0615925707
ISBN-10: 0615925707

©2013 Amana Mission Publishing Ink Alternative Press

Design and images by
Amana Mission All-In-One Media Magician

*If you would like to adapt any piece within this volume for musical composition or reprint, please contact us via e-mail at **ampi@amanamission.com***

More writing from Indi Riverflow abounds
*Please visit **www.amanamission.com** to stay current*

This volume is dedicated to my literary elders, who paved the path I now tread, all the mages of language who made possible the work I so love; and to those laboring now and in the future for the sake of the Great Work.

ALP --> HCE

Table of Context

Introspect

☿

Aporia Rhapsodia:
It's Not A Bug, It's A Feature

This is a book of riddles.

What are riddles? Riddles are portals to the unknown. Riddles are spectacles of perspective, conceptual illusions, speed traps along the roads of routine reasoning. Riddles are big concepts conveying themselves in small spaces. Riddles are behind the green glass door. Life is littered with riddles. Our lives are how we answer them.

Riddles bend the mind and defy expectations. Riddles are mental exercise, cognitive calisthenics promoting an agile intuition and supple imagination, flexing faculties of flexibility, stretching the edges of possibility.

Each day poses mundane riddles, static mysteries relating to the economics of time, space, and our place in them. These daily dilemmas reflect deeper enigmas, nested inside other mysteries, *ad infinitum*, which are framed by our own unique set of clues, providing texture to the collective quest.

We are engaged in a mad treasure hunt, with myriad conflicting maps in circulation, pursuing the elusive gold, unsure if we are seeking a trove of literal or metaphorical metal, or a cache of iron pyrite, or something else beyond comprehension.

So successful has the human animal been in resolving the natural puzzles of survival, and unsuccessful at resolving problems amongst ourselves, that our species has devised whole classes of activity devoted to the more dynamic inquiries troubling our hearts and minds.

Artists puzzle over the possibilities of a particular medium, submitting solutions born from the soul. When we dance, we are answering the unspoken riddle of how to match our movement to the music. When we create, we are solving the implicit riddle posed by our culture and personal viewpoint: what does the world require, which I might uniquely be able to offer?

All these individual inquiries are fractal refractions of the Grand Riddle: what is the nature of existence itself, and self in relation to the Cosmos? What am I for, and what shall I do?

Riddles beguile with obviousness, exposing faulty patterns and prejudiced thinking. The urge to slay the conceptual dragon brings out the deeply real limitations inherent to the habit of short-cuts we often miscall our thought.

The notorious and mysterious mischief of Mercury in retrograde, that periodic hailstorm of glitches, rapidly emerged as the compelling question driving this volume of verse, trailing in his orbital wake expansive meditations: on mythology, the paradoxes of parallax perspective, the alchemical transmutation of abstraction into action, cosmic trickery, and most particularly, the meaning of error.

What I find most curious about this apparent retrograde motion is the way it amounts to, in essence, an optical illusion; nothing happens to Mercury itself. Rather, the perception that any given planet's direction has reversed celestial course is produced by the relative position of the Earth. The whole effect is a trick of perspective.

There is no rational reason I can summon to explain why, in strictly physical terms, this astronomical anomaly should impact human affairs at all, let alone in the mildly disruptive fashion that is the hallmark of the Herald gone haywire.

If I were very inclined to a method of strict rationality, I should be forced to resort to dismissing the matter entirely, chalking any anecdotes off to "coincidence" or "confirmation bias" and filing the whole phenomenon in a mental trash bin marked, "superstitious nonsense," along with other such hoodoo notions.

I am not, however, one for holding too much stock by rational thought, as those who know me will be quick to attest. Vastly over-rated, suffocating straightjacket of a mentality, sanity is. And if there's one thing I've learned about writing, it is that typing in a straightjacket is pure madness.

"The time has come," the Walrus said, "to vacuum the downstairs ceiling."

Even hardened skeptics can be made to pale in terror under the barrage of cosmic error during Mercury retrograde. There were three such periods during 2013, a year which was rich in ironic reversals, and therefore fertile with material. The embryonic framework of this collection, based around the eponymous lyric, emerged during the first, in Pisces, was completely restructured during the middle phase, in Cancer, and once again, through Scorpio, in preparation for publication. This became intentional, but it didn't start that way.

There really is a Haywire Hill, so dubbed, and at first, I deeply regretted visiting that vortex of confusion. Without trotting out a complete laundry list of mishaps which struck us there during a few hectic days in early July, I will say that the experience was more than enough, for my purposes anyway, to remove the retrograde riddle from the realm of academic speculation, and place the matter squarely in the category of immediate survival.

Amana and I ventured to the small town of Felton in our bus, Mahayana, to help organize a giant vinyl record archive in advance of some upcoming storage transfers; it was a friendly favor. Or so we imagined.

The records belong to a fixture of the music scene, who we took to calling "the Walrus," for his handlebar mustache and eccentric manner.

Coo coo ca choo.

Mahayana is a Sanskrit word meaning "Great Vehicle," and this particular bus has served us well, having housed the headquarters of our laterally mobile publishing enterprise since inception. A converted church shuttle, often propelled and maintained by the power of prayer, Mahayana is not much of a mountain climber.

Like many semi-rural properties in Northern California, our destination was perched about a hundred feet above the graded road, at the top of a narrow dirt driveway. The hill looked innocuous enough, on cursory inspection in the waning daylight, but we hadn't reckoned on few factors: a steep grade just below the parking area, the mechanical limits of our old vehicle at such an angle bearing the weight load of a crash pad on wheels-or, naturally, Mercury being in retrograde.

Our bus began to roll helplessly backward, toward the vulnerable house and its screaming owner, mirroring Mercury in an all-too-material imitation of retrograde reversal. Forward progress abruptly ceased, just as we were about to maneuver into our berth, and the brakes blew out under the stress, abruptly powerless. Gravity had caught up to us in a big way.

The record collector fell, yelling helplessly under the rolling rear end of the immovable object. Wheels spun. We screamed, too. Multiple lives flashed before our collective eyes. What had we done?

The Walrus was fortunately unharmed, apart from a twisted ankle, but we now found ourselves perched in a precarious position, on several levels. The emergency brake prevented the bus from slipping out of control again, but the neighbors weren't fans of our impromptu parking job, and didn't seem to understand why we were hesitant to move again, no matter how we explained our alien value system and predicament.

We placed the survival of our vehicle and host's carport above their ability to use their usual parking spot; they, naturally, had an opposite perspective. I could see their point, but our spaceship was grounded and no amount of harassment could change that unpleasant reality.

The culture clash cascaded into a chain of chaos. A neighborly scuffle broke out over our refusal to relocate, and everything but the bus went downhill from there. The muscular inhabitant of the next parcel assumed a threatening demeanor against our increasingly distraught Walrus, who was now on crutches and unfortunately prone to making wild, swinging gestures with them in hand. Police were called, and called away again, through deft crisis management. Not one stack of records was packed that night.

This rapid streak of degenerating conditions took place within the first few hours on Haywire Hill. Then began the long, arduous quest to return the bus to flat and legally unthreatened parking. This entailed three more days of negotiating with tow operators, untold hours on the phone with roadside assistance, more bristling incidents with the hostile and unsympathetic neighbors, all while managing the un-mangled ankle of the Walrus, who was now limping inadvisedly around, cursing frequently and wondering what darkness we sorcerous pagans had brought to his quiet, phonographic retreat. The ostensible mission was devoured in the drama that followed our fateful decision to take on that damn hill.

The sky itself seemed to sigh relief when the ordeal came to an anticlimactic conclusion, following a nearly catastrophic and life-threatening brake failure, two visits from law enforcement, and four from various tow truck companies all bafflingly unable to unhook the Catch-22 we had maneuvered into.

When the dust settled, we were free from the quagmire, no serious damage done. We even had a reasonably accurate diagnosis of our brake issue from the brave tow driver, who had solved the problem by bucking regulations, taking the bus by the wheel and slowly rolling backward, in drive gear, all the way to level ground.

We were finally extracted from Haywire Hill, and I had some writing to do. Reckoning my fortune in glitches, I suddenly felt quite rich.

When traveling in higher dimensions, linear thought and action lead perpetually into peril. The way seems littered with obstacles. This applies to psychological topology as well geological terrain, for similar reasons.

At the end of the road, having learned to look and leap, these apparent barriers are revealed as stepping stones to another level of adaptation; the obstacles *were* the path.

You could say it felt like a miracle when things finally stopped going wrong.

At the very apogee of awareness, where magic and logic mingle, exist enigmas which tease the imagination, defy explanation, and add dimensions of perspective on our quick flight from womb to tomb.

Here is where dreams linger, epiphanies emerge, and vacuous visions find their way to paper and ink, becoming concrete for that brief interstice between the writing of words and reading of them.

This is where I prefer to bide, in the Magma mines along Pine Cone Ridge, contemplating by inner eye the ineffable strangeness of being, and doing my best to translate these hazy glimpses into streams of morphemes worthy of song.

Mmmm…morphemes…

I am, I must admit, thoroughly addicted to the stuff. I've had to enter the trade, just to keep my own supply flowing.

The highest quality morpheme mixes, containing the greatest degree of verity, are what I call "Magma." You know, the liquid *gold*. I hunt this Fool's Gold in the caverns of consciousness, in search of an angry fix for the broken babble plaguing our collective conversation.

Magma is what dogma once was, before freezing on

the windblown surface of the mind, ossifying through mindless repetition, becoming its own opposite. Magma is transformative and dynamic, underlying visible reality, and heedlessly incites insight when exposed to open air, until the flames cool and another Pompeii is erected upon it to await incineration.

Dogmas demand that subjective experience conform to some theoretical objective value system and framework, while Magma generates estimations, in constant revision, from the collective subjective. Dogma dictates a narrow path; Magma invents the need for new trails to be blazed in response to a shifting landscape.

Magma springs from rare and perilous peaks, founts of fiery inspiration and seer-ing wisdom. Magma is not carved in stone; the smoky signals can be read only from ephemeral wisps, spotted in the heat of the firewalk. Magma is eternally churning, burning old edifices to the ground, and forging the foundation of a new cultural landscape.

Culture is to minds what it is to microbes. Mentalities reared on the monocultures embodied by empirical modalities develop predictably, prosperous enough until confronted with contamination by Other. We have arrived at the limits of linearity; the world is awash in war predicated on very slight distinctions in cultural flavor.

The challenges of a global culture have added an edge of urgency to the age-old quest for understanding. Rigid religious and political ideologies violently bumping up against each other is increasingly intolerable in a nonlocal conceptual environment, where the despot's nudity can be posted with minute-by-minute accuracy for all to mock.

Dogmas offer the illusion of certainty. But Magma offers something infinitely more useful: the means to cope with sustained uncertainty.

It's a metaphor, of course. And what is the meta for? It became evident at one point on Haywire Hill that the languages of logic lacked the context for apprehending what was happening. Whatever the true cause of our frustrating chain of errors, what we needed was a *poetic* understanding of the phenomenon.

Mythical figures serve as a way to embody cosmic principles too complex for rational dissection. These archetypes arrange themselves into coherent pantheons through a transmigration of concept conveyed via the art of an age.

Mercury, known to Greeks as Hermes, is a fleet-footed mediator between states of being. Hermes is a busy deity, conducting messages from the gods and mortal souls to the underworld. He is the original author, having invented words, and progenitor of music, designing the first woodwinds and stringed instrument for Apollo.

Hermes, like most Olympian deities, is often portrayed as possessed of a questionable and mischievous character.

The wily one began his career with a prank, the theft of Apollo's prize herds. As the legend of liquid silver goes, the prodigious thief presented the lyre to Apollo in reparations, and song was born.

The lyre, an ancestor of the guitar made from guts and tortoise shell, was a device for poets, adding a melodic dimension to the highly structured odes, epics, and hymns conveying the events of the mythical dimension.

The seedy roots of rock n' roll are found in this tale, and wily Hermes is a central figure in my own personal mythos, a garrulous guide in the borderlands of consciousness, where scraps of resonance morph into semblances of messages across the rainbow bridge.

So the riddle remains: what is at the core of this mutating metaphor, held in your hands and holding your eyes? I must confess, the best either of us can do is guess, and the best you can do is set down the bread crumb trail of clues. For these pages have spun themselves from the ether, out of an endeavor I can only explain in terms of a fervent transmutation. They are songs, but I don't know how, or where, they will come to go. That is for the future to reveal.

Many modern culture consumers are prone to regard poetry as a child of the printed page, a quaint niche for the nostalgic, forgetting that verse forms are intended for the ear, containing implied cadences, emphases, and other dramatic flourishes interpreted uniquely in each rendering. This invisible element, along with the melody of musical adaptations, is supplied by whatever voice has captured it in the air, dynamic and collaborative.

Imagine, if you will, the tunes underlying these unsung songs ahead, and if you happen to strike musical gold, drop me a line via my publisher. Unless, of course, Mercury happens to be in retrograde; in that case, have my publisher contact you.

-ASAOS Hx3
Indi Riverflow

Strange Loops

I had this thought about a thought I had
I wondered what would happen if I said
I have this thought inside my head
About this thought about this thought I had

What I am about to tell you is true
But what I just said is a lie
Boomerang bouncin' back at you
In vicious circles of transparent dye

The origin is at its end
And the needle breeds the eye
The messenger is what it sends
Through the lens which bends the sky

There seems to be no way to know
If you can really know what I mean
If you've ever spied the spiral glow
Or even seen what I call green

Not sure what we're understanding
In this tangled plot
You might say it's almost nothing
But it's not

We're a story told in alphabet soup
With just enough ink to link the chain
Just a group of strange strange loops
That the void could not contain

The strangest part is this living thing
Hardly seems natural at all
Strings of code self-replicating
On this suspiciously habitable ball

Not sure what we're understanding
In this tangled plot
You might say it's almost nothing
But it's not

What I am about to tell you is true
But what I just said is a lie
Boomerang bouncin' back at you
In vicious circles of transparent dye

I had this thought inside my head
I wondered what would happen if I said
I had this thought inside my head
I wondered what would happen if I said

Liquid Silver

Music by John Kadlecik
First performed by JKB 3-28-2014

A wild one born with no time to waste
Wings on his shoes and ready to race
Got up to play on his first day of birth
Full of fast ones to lay on the Earth

Son of the thunder by a quiet girl
Slick little trickster took off in a whirl
Trouble to make and chains to yank
By dusk pulling off his first epic prank

The Sun awoke one ancient dawn
To learn his happy herds were gone
The tracks were fresh the trail was clear
But the thief and steer were nowhere near

Quick as liquid silver
In a position second to none
We've only just begun to run
Backward circle, circle backward
Backward circles around the Sun

Tracking down the culprit didn't take long
But instead of a tantrum the brat burst into song
A hymn to memory's gold-drenched glories
Retelling each detail of the Sun's own story

Say, let me make my amends with this lyre
Brother I'm thrilled to find you inspired
Your goodwill is worth a great deal
More than any wealth I might ever steal

Wherefore this sound from the tortoise shell
How the hell do you make it sing so well?
Well, I don't know but I think it's gonna grow
Into the groove and guts of rock and roll

Quick as liquid silver
In a position second to none
We've only just begun to run
Backward circle, circle backward
Backward circles around the Sun

Renaissance of Resonance

Let's grab a sip of novel tea
And swing from the limbs of realitree
Well shift happens
When we're all fluxed up
So bring out your brilliance
And let's raise our cups
To the Renaissance of resonance

The golden balance is bound to be found
Answers will always come around
It worked back then it'll work again
If the principle is sound

It might be more realistic
To remain pessimistic
But it's better to be happy than right
And I'd rather figure out how we might
Turn the stern of this panic-wracked Titanic
Try to incite or at least invite
A lifeboat to float our finest insight

The golden balance is bound to be found
Answers will always come around
It worked back then it'll work again
If the principle is sound

It's an age of mass confusion
Setting the stage for revolution
Bit by bit and byte by byte
Lighting up the edge of evolution
But all some eyes desire
Is the starkness of night
However mighty the bonfire
The Titan's scorching torch ignites

The golden balance is bound to be found
Answers will always come around
It worked back then it'll work again
If the principle is sound

Imagineering by intuition
Teasing the future into fruition
On plateaus of punmanteaus
Lining winding cascading tableaus
Of shining stars on a mission
Rise up as visionaries always arose
It's half past time your talent shows

Corporate Logos

You know the flow by where it won't go
Outlines define shapes of the signs
Drawn in the span between high tide and low
Visible only when moonlight shines
Digging and ditching double-edged duality
Emulating every enemy
As we go about the business
Of rebranding reality

Spiraling staircase spells out the word
That all eyes know and no ears have heard
Four letters in the flesh
Swirling in a soup
Strangely stirred
Walking the talk
Stumbling and slurred

Banks of currency backed by trust
Storing the solid light of the sun
An interest rate which self-adjusts
And long lines of numbers which add up to one
Accounts inherited by birthright of dust
With a perpetual balance of all and none

Making matters in our own hands
Building by blueprints in sand
With the endless supply of endless demand
Swimming in the subspace substrate
Creation in search of something to create
Anagrams and amalgamated visions
Fused by the art of inverted fission

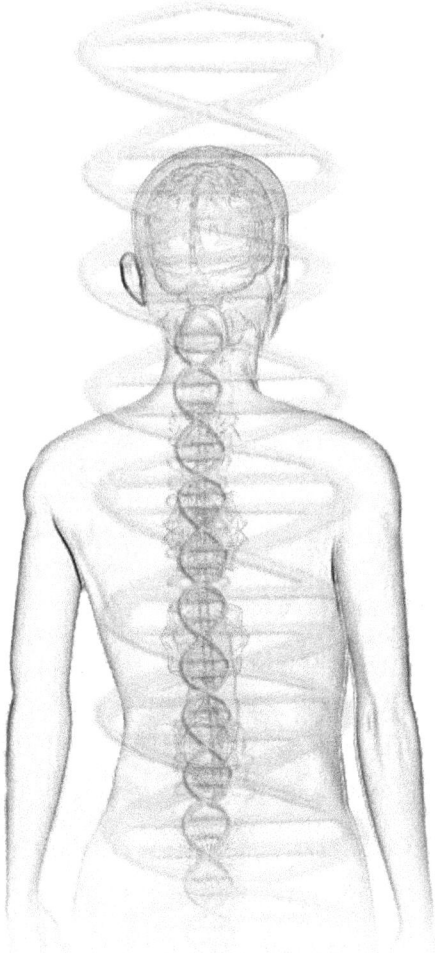

The Great Vehicle

Deadicated to the Intrepid Trippers of Furthur
First performed by JKB 3-28-2014
Music by John Kadlecik

Roll that rock up the slope once more
Falls every time but who's keeping score?
The higher we push, the tougher it grows
I built this, Sisyphus, so I know how it goes

The road is a riddle, it sometimes seems
Muddle through the middle or edge the extremes?
Smile all the miles in my burnt-out machine
Just to move the movie on to the next scene

We all get to give
What we've been given
Take our turns
Driving and being driven
One incarnation under façade
Invisibly indivisible
The ride of our lives
On board the Great Vehicle
We are the bus and the bus is us

Rising to the rare air above it all
To glimpse a world without any walls
Hung in a harness strung from worn threads
Held in the dreams of my unsteady head

The mountaintop can be a cold, lonely spot
Calling out to other dots out of earshot
Divinity is deafening, so back to the ground
To bring to the valley all the visions I found

The trip back down is an artful slide
Some slip in the rush and crack open wide
Wild-eyed wrecks unable to land
Babbling in tongues none can understand

We all get to give
What we've been given
Take our turns at the wheel
Driving and being driven
One incarnation under façade
Invisibly indivisible
The ride of our lives
On board the Great Vehicle

We are the bus and the bus is us
We are the bus and the bus is us
We are the bus and the bus is us
We are the bus and the bus is us

Flight Plans

I've heard it many times observed
It's all in how you take the curves
Every storm you swerve
Just more fire for the nerves

Running down the oily runway
Waylaid by connection delays
Swinging signs of wired semaphore
Wringing hands of tired metaphor

It's hard to hear you down on the ground
While you fly by at the speed of sound
Could have sworn this was a stop on your list
But in all the noise I must have missed this

We all sometimes arrive a little late
And we all leave someone hangin' at the gate
At least I'm piling my frequent crier miles
Won't you pardon me while
I go repaint my smile

Patience might be quite the virtue
I guess its feels like I'm chasing curfew
And maybe I get caught up in the rush
But if I don't I'll be slammed in the crush

Now if we made our successes
The way we make our excuses
We'd be right now on a flight bound for Mars
A pit stop on our way to some new-found stars

We all sometimes arrive a little late
And we all leave someone hangin' at the gate
At least I'm piling my frequent crier miles
Won't you pardon me while
I go repaint my smile

All the rules say to cool my jets
But not a year has made me younger yet
On the nonstop red-eye from the womb to the tomb
You'll know where I was by the subsonic boom
Yeah, you'll know where I was by the subsonic boom

Wax and String

I get my best work done in my sleep
Last night I made a mountain
That would make Olympus weep
Rode up there on a fountain
From a well ten miles deep
Found a fresh new planet to live on
A world we'll have the wit to keep

Caught a comet out to Saturn's rings
Where I had some Titans to meet
Zipped out by Jove to flex my wings
Waxen and weightless and fleet
Showed off my moves to some old dead kings
And when I felt bold enough to meet the heat
I dove directly into the source of things

Takes a lot for wax and strings
To fly away with freedom
Oh you've got the wings
But have you got the wisdom?

And if I have hold of one regret
As I tumble back to Earth in confusion
I suppose I wish I had laid my bets
Reckoning the power of hydrofusion
If only we'd weighed the real threats
Of flight by a child of the dungeon
All the things I haven't learned yet
Beyond the reach of resolution

Takes a lot for wax and strings
To fly away with freedom
Oh you've got the wings
But have you got the wisdom?

In this game of musical stairs
All is lost if you're stuck in a chair
As we contemplate compromising
The fire is below and quickly rising
The only way out is up in the air
Take the elevator all the way to the top
When you get there just forget to stop
Take the elevator all the way to the top
When you get there just forget to stop

Lonesome Blues

Kicking rocks off the loading docks
Counting this one off to hard knocks
Symbols of you sinking from sight
Slipping away in ripples of spite
My eyes are bone dry, but I won't lie
This ocean here was a desert last night

It was love at first fantasy
We had matching plates of vanity
Flashy accents of eccentricity
And equal love for lunacy
You had tons of talent and all the right stats
But integrity, or loyalty
Or whatever you'd call that quality
No, you didn't have a lick of that
Now I see, through the light under the door
That's all I ought to have been looking for

It must comfort the confused
Laughing as we lose
I hope they are amused
By my bitter lonesome blues

I have this way of seeing
People in the way I wanted to see
And you have this way of being
What people want you to be
So for a sober second's rest
Around an aching heart
I agree, it probably is for the best
That we pursue our illusions apart

It must comfort the confused
Laughing as we lose
I hope they are amused
By my bitter lonesome blues

In every mansion that burns
There's always something to learn
Sifting through ashes to track
The bonfire back to the spark
As I comb through my fears
I come back to the mirror
Shattered and hollow and empty and dark

Feedback

I can't tell what's left or right
Which way is up or down
If I've hit a dangerous height
Or if we're grazing near the ground
Can't see where we're heading
If it's back to where I've been
Since I'm flyin' blind
If you'd be so kind
Open a line and fill me in
Please open a line and fill me in

Static from this feedback loop
Sounds exactly like your voice
I keep asking myself
What are the chances of a choice?

Hit the dunes without a guide
Or compass to point the way
The buggy I had hoped to ride
Became a burden to convey
The footing keeps sliding
Buried up to my chin
Since I'm in a bind
If you wouldn't mind
Toss me a line and bring me in
Won't you toss me a line and bring me in?

While you wait I must bide
Hanging limbo without a stick
On the other side of our steep divide
And the trail's getting slick
If I had my way it'd be yesterday
Cause this doubt is wearing thin
But I'd settle for a sign
Just few feet of vine
Or a scrap of twine to tie me in
Yeah, a scrap of twine to tie me in

Static from this feedback loop
Sounds exactly like your voice
I keep asking myself
What are the chances of a choice?

Drifting now and falling free
Frozen with all this liberty
Are we in space or are we at sea?
Sailing under veils of uncertainty
Wavering grip keeps slipping
Gravity wants to win
It's quite a grind
So if you find the time
Shoot me a line and clue me in
Now won't you shoot me a line and clue me in?

Transitive Venus

I tried dating a painting
All hung-up from where I sat
Found me most unfit for framing
And all my jokes were fallin' flat

Started seeing a statue
But I knew it wouldn't last
Stuck up on that pedestal
And going nowhere fast

Waiting for the Transitive Venus
Lit with star-crossed designs
Nothing to come between us
When our charts and hearts align

Sank into a soft silken pillow
Thinking there I might rest my head
But beneath it was a crossbow
Set for a battle in that bed

Always fell for that fatal arrow
And rose again for another shot
Hunting hearts among the shadows
We're the only game we've got

Waiting for the Transitive Venus
Lit with star-crossed designs
Nothing to come between us
When our charts and hearts align

Only twice a century a pair
Arrives at such perfection
A fleeting flirtation so rare
It fuels all other flares of affection

Riverrun

Music by John Kadlecik
First performed by JKB 3-28-2014

Well, I come bearing an hourglass
Where the sand flows both ways
Not very clear on matters of mass
But quite precise on how energy plays
Remember the future about like the past
Clouded by how much I'm missing today
All I can say is both move very fast
And in the slowest of all possible ways

From swerve of shore
To bend of bay
Ending up where it was once begun
A way a lone a last a loved
Along the riverrun

I find my way by ballpoint compass
'Cause my world is mapped on a sphere
Needle tuned to the heart of bliss
Nested in a maze of ten billion gears
Right now it's pointing directly at this
Voyage of thought on waves to your ears
As a sailor who knows it's so easy to miss
Islands of hope in storms of fear

From swerve of shore
To bend of bay
Ending up where it was once begun
A way a lone a last a loved
Along the riverrun

Half of humanity is planted on Earth
So the rest can sculpt the sky
Someone must keep the sense of mirth
In a mound of molasses ten miles high
In the intermission 'tween death and birth
We get to be ghosts with the freedom to fly
Relearn what a good limitation is worth
The way you dig on a well gone suddenly dry

From swerve of shore
To bend of bay
Ending up where it was once begun
A way a lone a last a loved
Along the riverrun

Pine Cone Ridge

Trap doors in shifting floors
As I tumble from the sky
Where half a blink before
I swear I knew how to fly

I come from the vista
Of the inside eye
Where gravity's just a
Local rule to defy

Iris left you a message
At the edge of rainbow bridge
Spelled out in the language of images
Turn in at the signs along Pine Cone Ridge

There's just a half-step of separation
Dividing diamond-faced dimensions
Tinsel filaments of reflection
Lost in transit and translation

Wispy scattered glimmers
Frames flipped out of sequence
Stirring a mixture of pictures
Chronicling inverted events

Iris left you a message
At the edge of rainbow bridge
Spelled out in the language of images
Turn in at the signs along Pine Cone Ridge

Greeting degrees of gradation
Along the spectrum of sensation
Riding rails of radiation
Through the tunnels of perception

Smoke drifting away
Firmament's gone quaking
Fading fast into the day
Beneath the weight of waking

Iris left you a message
At the edge of rainbow bridge
Spelled out in the language of images
Turn in at the signs along Pine Cone Ridge

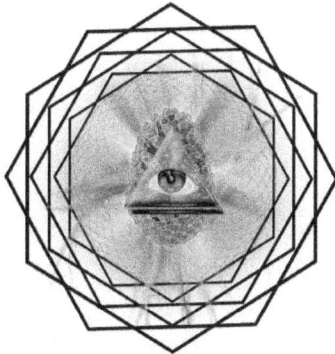

Lattice of Errors

The first thing I ever learned about plans
Is that you'd better factor in the glitch
Expeditions hanging on human hands
Rarely return without a hitch

Two wrongs don't make a right
But sometimes three lefts do
Survival has struck again despite
Every rift I slipped clear through

Sometimes you've got to let go and fall free
Land in the net of serendipity
I've seen mountaineers crumble in terror
Afraid to gamble all on a guess
I'll just climb my lattice of errors
And make an impeccable mess

Navigating shaky terrain and tricky gaps
Takes special tools and luck of the Fool
Making magic out of mishaps
When the tether snaps on the end of the spool

You never can know what fate you missed
Imps at your heels and keeping you late
Spin you around with a synchronous twist
Away from whatever was due on that date

Sometimes you've got to let go and fall free
Land in the net of serendipity
I've seen mountaineers crumble in terror
Afraid to gamble all on a guess
I'll just climb my lattice of errors
And make an impeccable mess

So take it with a grain of philosophy
If you've grooved yourself hard into a ditch
You paid for the lesson in catastrophe
Value hard knocks and you'll always be rich

Sometimes you've got to let go and fall free
Land in the net of serendipity
I've seen mountaineers crumble in terror
Afraid to gamble all on a guess
I'll just climb my lattice of errors
And make an impeccable mess

Dimension Not Available

A birthday ode to Douglas Noel Adams, so long and thanks for all the laughs...

When touring the Galaxy remember these tips
Only the very strange seem to survive the trip
Never mind sudden shifts of gravity and reality
Be sure you're well prepared for bad alien poetry

There are days you wake up to find out
Your world's in the path of an interstellar route
You could wallow in doom and drown in despair
Or get out the Guide to see what remains out there

Learning to fly
Is a trick as easy as pie
The secret's simply this:
Fling yourself at the Earth and miss

Ship you've hitched seems the worst possible place
And then you're tossed to the void of outer space
The irony-laden Universe is infinitely perverse
Just don't panic, 'cause it can always get worse

And the President's a Three-Faced Hustler
A shameless stud and spaceship rustler
Once you get used to the lay of the Milky Way
Just like home, the Galaxy's governed by clichés

Learning to fly
Is a trick as easy as pie
The secret's simply this:
Fling yourself at the Earth and miss

You can let an awful lot of little things slide
If you are improbable enough to snag a ride
All you need is a towel and a golden heart
But it helps to read multidimensional charts

Comic justice is the only fair kind
In a Cosmos where we're all flying blind
The answer is forty-two my friend
What did you say the question was again?

Extensible Now

Tingling with tension
And apprehension
On the edge of invention
A hundred miles high

Automatic cognition
Tuned to transmissions
Material vision
Appears in the sky

The never-ending telling
Of the eternal Tao
In the plastic elastic
Extensible now

Clouds of confusion
Rain resolutions
Elusive illusions
Hanging by a hair

Engaged evolution
Evoking solutions
Concrete abstractions
Molded in the mirror

Reflecting impressions
Of passing perceptions
Defying expression
But coming quite near

The never-ending telling
Of the eternal Tao
In the plastic elastic
Extensible now

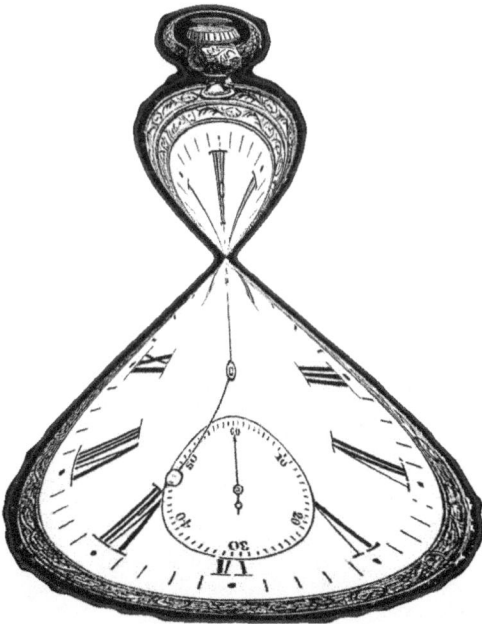

Down to Delphi

Quite a crowd at Muse's Mountain
Line winding well beyond the horizon
For a fleeting peek behind time's curtain
And they're emerging looking
Even more uncertain

They come to banish their blues
Collecting useless cryptic clues
Catch a sketch of tomorrow's news
No answer makes sense when
The question's confused

Down to Delphi
For a spot of riddles and rye
Down to Delphi
Answers never seem to apply
Down to Delphi
Advice you're bound to defy
Down to Delphi
Whatever they try to prophesy

I sat at the feet of the Oracle
In a resplendent crystal hall
Stream of movement seemed to stall
Cascading scenes of imagining
Reflecting on the walls

I will try to relate the explanation
Of how we created all creation
The only true gold is information
Matter's not the particles
It's in their relation
It's in their relation
It's in their relation

Green Glass Door

You'll find puzzles but no pieces
Losslessness but no increases
Shuffled illusion which never ceases
From jugglers tossing without releases

There are riddles but no clues
There are feet untouched by shoes
There is narrative but no true news
Smoothest jazz but no rhythm or blues

We see challenges but no victory
Dilemmas but no adversity
Appearances but no live audition
Illumination but no real vision

We find symmetry but no symbols
Booming bass but not a trace of treble
Omissions but no startling glare
Between the lines that aren't there

There is different but no same
Acclaim but no fame
Glitter but no glamor
Behind the green glass door

There are ballots but no leaders
There are books but no readers
Rabble but no revolutions
Many guesses but no solutions

There is spelling but no meaning
Yelling but no understanding
And telling but no showing
Rebelling but no uniting

There is happening but no action
And fulfillment, but no satisfaction
There is seeking but nothing to find
Intelligence but there is no mind
Oh who knows what lies behind
The glorious green glass door?

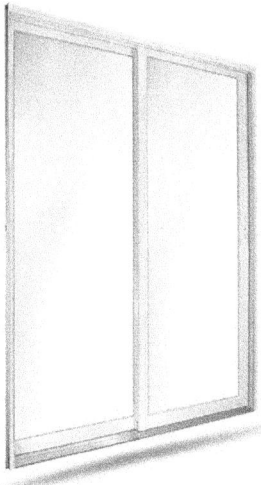

Tastelessly Tongue-Tied

By now you'd think that I'd have brought
Some erudite or at least clever thought
Some compelling gem, sparkling and rare
Or a little bit of that rapier wit
To slice the heavy atmosphere

You'd think I'd have an epic line writ
To fill pregnant pauses of dead air
Hanging in a moment too small to fit
All the words which ought to be there

A little late with the hip and humble
The laugh's been born and died
While I stumble and mumble
Struck dumbly mum and tastelessly tongue-tied
Tastelessly tongue-tied

You'd think by now I'd have clear in my head
All the impatient ideas in line to be said
A sense of the essential and sublime
Or crack of levity to lighten the lead
And suspend the gravity of time

A little late with the hip and humble
The laugh's been born and died
While I stumble and mumble
Struck dumbly mum and tastelessly tongue-tied
Tastelessly tongue-tied

Oh, you'd think I'd have blazing insights
Always ready to drop on a dime
But I'm simply speechless in the spotlights
Right when I'd best be at my prime

And if I'd had my wits about me
If I had that moment to revise
Instead of uttering inanities
I might have stayed silent and wise

A little late with the hip and humble
The laugh's been born and died
While I stumble and mumble
Struck dumbly mum and tastelessly tongue-tied
Tastelessly tongue-tied

Magnetism

If you're looking for sunshine
But forgetting the rain
If you're blinded by fire
To pitfalls and pain
If you are driven by desire
And conquests to gain

You're making moves on mere mist
That cannot be kissed
She can't be won
Because she doesn't exist

If you are seeking a secret
The code's long since cracked
Just be as magnetic as the magnet
You want to attract

When the race seems
Designed to deny victory
Even the meekest of dreams
Are dust on delivery
Chasing space
And tending insecurities
Aiming arrows at sparrows
While blind to the gold
That glitters only in the light
Of the bright and the bold

It's a dance with masks
Where we flirt through lies
Anyone who asks
Defies the disguise
Diverted down into
Dark empty dead ends
Not a trace left of you
In the wind of pretend

It may be battle
Or it may be a game
High duels of drama
And low cruel shifting shame
Downing in drink
Or burnt out by blame
If you aren't ready
She'll be the same

If you are seeking a secret
The code's long since cracked
Just be as magnetic as the magnet
You want to attract

Amazing as the magnet
You want to attract

Mark of the Djinn

If I bow my head
When I walk into the wind
My hat won't fly off

I am the eternal presence of air
I am the mad driver
Jumping cliffs on a dare
I am wind-whipped voices
Vaulting visceral visages
Painting invisible silhouettes
Across abstract ridges

Climb the peak you were born to scale
Cross the ocean you came here to sail
Cut-rate discounts on holy grails
We're only in it to help blaze the trail

The secret is there isn't one
We're woven into every wild yarn spun
We may not be mastered
Our treasure is free
Wish at your own hazard
For downsides are tough to see
Plenty of spirits for us all to drink
That bottle of Djinn holds more than you think

Climb the peak you were born to scale
Cross the ocean you came here to sail
Cut-rate discounts on holy grails
We're only in it to help blaze the trail

We'll tend to lend
Color to your grey
And flavors to your mythic buffets
But art is just another part we play
When the game is old we just go away
And let our echoes have their say
Dependable as those bells ringing in a new day

Djinn You Win

See, you rubbed the lamp so now I am bound
To awaken you like a tireless hound
My light cannot be partly revealed
Illumination begins with the yielded shield

I am embedded in the code of love
As it is below, so it must be above
I am evoked by the surrender of will
To principles which can never be killed

It's not a test
There's no right question
It's about the quest
Not the destination

Riddle me this, o impudent man
Who sought to place me under command
What's your plan to understand
The forces thus released by your hand?

Church rats scurry and old moths flutter
In corridors full of cobwebs and clutter
As ancient heads inaudibly mutter
In whispers from across the shutter

You want to brew success
I'll give you this simple recipe
Equal measures or your best guess
Of everything destiny drove you to be
All that honor demands and no less
Plenty of improvised integrity
Drop in a dash of dignity
And just a touch
Not too much
Of spicy subtlety

It's not a test
There's no right question
It's about the quest
Not the destination

Inherit the Djinn

There were many fine intentions
A long line of honorable mentions
Who for reasons most unclear to me
Decided that something like me should be
Be a gracious good host now
Now don't think about how
How to tender the phrase of the day
Just open up and get out of the way

Our ways are legion
In the legacy of each age
Sifting through circuits of sinner and sage
Inherit the Djinn
In a whirl of cryptic will
Written in waves of wind

We are invoked in the spin of dance
Provoked by a trip deep down into trance
Mind unconfined by map or clock
Animating pathways unblocked and unlocked
Rhythm tapped out in secret knocks
Nocturnal netherworlds shimmer in shock
Oscillating rivers of resonance
Delivering dreamers their inheritance

Our ways are legion
In the legacy of each age
Sifting through circuits of sinner and sage
Inherit the Djinn
In a whirl of cryptic will
Written in waves of wind

The mortal span is a flash in the pan
Spread out in an ever-expanding fan
Tracing the grooves in which we move
Replacing the faces the reaper removes
Channels called to serve one and all
Always awakened and fully enthralled
Following the flow of least resistance
In those who know their ethereal inheritance

Rhapsody in Retrograde

Quite a crisis on Haywire Hill
By now we ought to know the drill
It's enough to make old Murphy ill
Any glitch which can pop up probably will

We're in the eye of a psychic cyclone
Yes, it's a mess, and you're not alone
Regroup until the stormwinds have blown
Retrograde wrinkles all that is known

The state of fate appears a bit perverse
As if we're under a curious curse
Maybe it's Mercury orbiting reverse
Or maybe it's the rest of the Universe

You know, this messenger's mission
Is subject to being suddenly spun
Mishaps always chancin' to happen
While I'm chasing Sun under the gun

Say, this empty bag weighs a ton
I'd love to chat, but I'd better run
You may not like the prize you won
Please don't shoot, I've only begun

The payment is tendered in verse
Sent in the form of reality checks
Not nearly enough to stuff a purse
But better tips than the service reflects

I brought my thoughts to the mail slot
Dropped in my cryptic bits of W.A.S.T.E.
Triple-stamped in care of all I'm not
With a request for the greatest haste
Drafts which couldn't face
Getting replaced
Covered with clues
From who knows who
And tales of ordeals
I somehow outpaced

Rhapsody in Retrograde
Cavalcade of escapades
Rhapsody in Retrograde
Promenade of plans mislaid
Rhapsody in Retrograde
Serenades for renegades

The state of fate appears a bit perverse
As if we're under a curious curse
Maybe it's Mercury orbiting reverse
Or maybe it's the rest of the Universe

Cassandra's Complex

Lydia and Troy were on top of the game
Perfectly perched to run the whole scene
They had fingers in every pie that came by
Yet managed to keep their hands clean

But after a while the service and smiles
Slowly declined while business boomed
The stacks and sacks were stacked in piles
Too high to see that danger loomed

It's a Trojan horse of course of course
'Cause traps are always too good to be true
It always goes south on a careless mouth
And a greedy soul wanting more than is due

Cassandra woke one day bathed in sweat
Tripping over her words in fright
For she had a vision of a closing net
Sweeping her complex in the night

In vain she tried to explain
How all this gold was doomed
None of them wanted to hear her complain
As the tape rolled on in the next room

It's a Trojan horse of course of course
'Cause traps are always too good to be true
It always goes south on a careless mouth
And a greedy soul wanting more than is due

You never feel like thinking twice
When they offer you twice the price
But you really ought to have second thoughts
About Greeks bearing gifts
And how Troy got caught

You ain't got to be no prophet
To see the wiring in the walls
Just take a look at the history books
The big ballers always fall

Mule's Gold

I'm a broker by day
Even broker by night
We deal in shades of grey
Green fading into white

Delivery's done, fortune's won
Pockets stuffed with burning dough
Another run under the gun
Just a little less than I owe

I'd sell you my soul
But it's already sold
Traded to the trolls
For some shiny Mule's Gold

Zipping at the speed of need
Where desperation drips
Sucking poisoned seeds of greed
On the short side of the flip

Can't spare a second to sniff the roses
There's enough cocaine
On this here plane
To numb ten million noses

I'd sell you my soul
But it's already sold
Traded to the trolls
For some shiny Mule's Gold

This business of chemistry
It's all a thin-lined blur
The edge of integrity
Where sleight of mind occurs

So if I loosen my collar
It's 'cause this heat is a drag
Bet doughnuts to dollars
It'll be me with the bag

Prisoner's Dilemma

The game getting grim and gruff
The men in suits shuffled me in
Talking tough and full of bluff
Down for a round of no one wins

They sat me down at the table
And laid me out the stakes
They told me they might be able
To cut me a lucky break

Please, please, please don't you plead
No, please, please, please don't you plead
I swear we'll all be freed
So please, please, please don't you plead

Man said, let me relieve your doubt
Save us all a little time
There's no more point in holding out
Your friends, they dropped the dime

Now I'd lay your cards down loose
Before the deal comes round again
Cause the guilty ones draw a deuce
But the innocent get sent for ten

Our lives reduced to poker chips
Sweat's thick enough to drown
If so much as a single words slips
House of cards comes tumbling down

Said, no, sir, I'll take my odds
You can keep your devil's deals
As I prayed to all the gods
Every lip stays zipped and sealed

Please, please, please don't you plead
No, please, please, please don't you plead
I swear we'll all be freed
So please, please, please don't you plead

Transmigrant Blues

Metempsychosis is a mental state where immortal
entities entertain delusions of mortality...

I met him pike hoses
In protean pantomimes
One door opens
As another one closes
One bell silenced
As another one chimes

Just a fresh headline
On the same old news
Returning from the churning
Burning with yearning
And singing the Transmigrant Blues

I dwell in Dedalus
Labryinthan odysseys
Shipwrecked galleys
Calypso circuities
Short times of space
Through short spaces of time

Just a fresh headline
On the same old news
Returning from the churning
Burning with yearning
And singing the Transmigrant Blues

Doublin' down instructions
In parallax constructions
Morphing intertextuality
Modalities of ineluction
Blooming into founts
Of epiphany in the first degree
And unnumbered counts
Of unmitigated premeditated poetry

Just a fresh headline
On the same old news
Returning from the churning
Burning with yearning
And singing the Transmigrant Blues

I am the Cyclops
I am no one
I am everyone

Ideas have immortality
If they deserve to survive
Authoring the authority
From which all tall walls derive
Grading shades of solubility
And which medium shall thrive
Shouting over the triviality
That usually consumes our lives

Led Tritely

Look for the bread crumb trail to follow
There's a rule of thumb for every sorrow
Don't reinvent the proverbial wheel
For what a dabbler dutifully borrows
The master shamelessly steals

Years come and go in a blink
Toss another stone in the soup
And see if it sinks

Bites of sound be here when we're gone
Dependable as tomorrow's dawn
Yeah, you know what they always say
Led tritely through the land of the living cliché

Pride goes before a fall
Warnings scrawled
On crumbling walls
I know you've heard that old saw
It applies to us all
Meals of crow tend to stick in the craw

Impact always comes rumbling back
Duck and cover in the pre-storm calm
Folks who live in diamond jack shacks
Shouldn't toss gravity bombs

Bites of sound be here when we're gone
Dependable as tomorrow's dawn
Yeah, you know what they always say
Led tritely through the land of the living cliché

Signs of symmetry
Our common currency
Adages maximized
Updated restated
And routinely revised
Scraps of script
Insights improvised
Catch-phrases compromised
Mediums of exchange
Mottoes of the free range
Some things never do change
Yeah, some things never do change

Bites of sound be here when we're gone
Dependable as tomorrow's dawn
Yeah, you know what they always say
Led tritely through the land of the living cliché

Sandals In A Haystack

We all bring our masks to the masquerade
Inventing characters to play the charade
Some are wrapped up tight in the groove
Some keep wry eyes on each other's moves

Some came here to play a game of chance
Some came merely to display their dance
Some came to stare in childlike awe
And scrapbook all the colors they saw

Sandals in a haystack
And tons of loose screws
You know it's a good party
When you lose your shoes

A limping love will sputter and die
Even as a new romance gathers sparks
Ten more collapse in stutters and lies
For every storybook ending that starts

Some will whither and shiver
Some will be bathed in heat
For some Fate will deliver
The trickiest kind of treat

Sandals in a haystack
And tons of loose screws
You know it's a good party
When you lose your shoes

Whatever you came hunting for
I wish you the best of luck, my friend
But all I am able to offer
Is what the music chooses to send

At the end of the night
When all is said and done
If we led any love into the light
This round of the game's been won

I Just Work Here

Putting out brushfires
As you spark another blaze
Tangled up in cross-haired wires
Yet the gilded guitar still plays

And here's an empty echo chamber
Compounding sounds of borrowed voices
No hooks in sight to serve as anchor
For your tapestry of choices

Gifted you are, oh yes it is true
But the gift was not meant only for you
We all chipped in to give you your due

Juggling jaws
Grasping straws
Struggling to claw
Free from the fame
Chained like a half-tame
Trained dancing bear
Don't blame me
I just work here

Pulled in six directions
Away from your beating heart
Split up in scattered sections
Sacrificed on the altar of art

Don't blame me
I just work here

I can see your rising ire
Bright as any flame
The sting from your cold shoulder
Burns me just the same

Don't blame me
I just work here

Oh I know if the roles reversed
I might roll my eyes like you
For I surely haven't seen the worst
Of what you're going through
Don't blame me
I just work here

Legend's End

I have traveled the trails of spice
For visions that struck me blind
I've twice toured the veils of vice
For a glance at virtues cloaked behind

I've sailed to the center of the Sun and back
Embarked on many fruitless quests
Searching for heroes in a haystack
As flames were blazing in the firebird's nest

I have seen a sea of heartless harpies
Shred a sailor's soul to ribbons
My blood is quite rich in irony
So my laughter might be forgiven

Bounding round the bend
When tenses and senses
Blur and blend
Where tale and teller
Together transcend
At the legend's end

I've fallen in and out of countless traps
Along the way to buried treasure
I've found and lost more ancient maps
Than I even know how to measure

Stories are what the sunshine becomes
Eroded to the speed of solid concrete
Pulsing out rhythms of phantom atoms
Bouncing to the beat of galactic heat

Bounding round the bend
When tenses and senses
Blur and blend
Where tale and teller
Together transcend
At the legend's end

Mandrake Lake

You know we had some bright nights
Down by Mandrake Lake
Dreamwebs dropped from swan-drawn flight
Waves of wakening washed in the wake

She whispers her will on the wisp of the wind
Ballets of fireflies and star-studded skies
Folds of old fables and worn yarns of the wise

You know we spied the deep inside
Floating in Mandrake Lake
Refracted reactions unable to hide
Mirrored in murmurs mortal mouths make

Freed from gravity by the heat of a candle
Cranked up with levity by a fiery handle
Hanging from a mile-high balloon

You know we drowned on what we found
Sinking into Mandrake Lake
Coiling cords around twilight sounds
Memory of water melting matter's mistakes

I might be a cracked broken vessel
Letting the stream slip and spill
Something's bound to break when you wrestle
With wit in the grip of wide-eyed will

You know we dove to the treasure trove
Beneath the surface of Mandrake Lake
Sprites in spite of the web we wove
When we wrested ourselves awake

Wizardry

Flexing that flexibility
As the map again unwraps
Sensing that some sensibilities
Carve impassable gaps

Straining every ability
Running on the last synapse
Juggling probabilities
Unsure how they'll collapse

It might be wizardry
But don't you think it's easy
It never looks like magic
On the inside of the trick

Sitting in the crucible
We're cranking up the gas
Down to bare essentials
Never mind the mass

Handling the invisible
Presents a unique set of needs
What you once thought conceptual
Bounces back at bullet speed

It might be wizardry
But don't you think it's easy
It never looks like magic
On the inside of the trick

Alchemy is all about purity
Dialing down the ego noise
Bar rises higher with every degree
That the firewalk destroys

It might be wizardry
But don't you think it's easy
It never looks like magic
On the inside of the trick

Hook and Nail

I have a tale of two twins
Orphans split up at birth
As opposite as yang and yin
As different as sky and Earth

One was sent off to a tower
Made of ivory and jade
To be taught the tools of power
And the rules of forging blades

The other twin was tossed aside
Hobbled by a twisted spine
Cast on a raft to ride out the tide
And vanish from the grand design

This is the tale of the hook and the nail
The endless regress of more or less
Answer from guess
And visions of veils

Raised by a school of sirens
The hunchback pored over questions
Melodious genuflections
Heading in any direction

The other grew to an upright citizen
And asking questions was a sin
Knew just how many seraphim
Could crowd on the point of a pin

This is the tale of the hook and the nail
The endless regress of more or less
Answer from guess
And visions of veils

Exclamation army
Firing at will
Aiming at truths
That just won't stand still

Hunchback huddle
Pondering puddles
Slippery and subtle
And eternally unfilled

Whether Vain

Too many cooks in this crowded kitchen
Don't even have a clue
All the seasoning you're pitchin'
Into my hoodoo stew

Don't try to be me
And I won't try to be you
I'm mixing the recipe
And I'm fixing this brew

You missed your cue, so hold your say
On every damn twist
That didn't turn your way
Rage the weather in your domain
Just please don't rain
On my hurricane

Got to slam the hammer down
Before the cloudy skies transform
Strike the nail into the crown
While the irony's still warm

Driving colliding pressure zones
To whip up thunder's form
Listening for the wind's whistling tone
To summon up the perfect storm

You skipped the script, so hold your say
On every damn twist
That doesn't turn your way
Mage the weather in your domain
Just please don't rain
On my hurricane

You'd try to fly before you could walk
Write a book before learning to talk
If you'd only learn to wait your turn
There's no Empire your fire can't burn

Golden Apple

Once a couple withheld an invitation
From Eris due to Her bad reputation
They wanted to have a quiet affair
And thought it was best if She wasn't there

The Goddess of Discord took great offense
Tired of always being barred from events
Social calendar in complete disarray
With nothing at all to do on that day

Should have invited Her to the wedding
Chaos is coming either way
Like a pile of unmade bedding
It'll get messed up anyway

Eris hatched a scheme to incite
The most mythically epic cat-scratch fight
Over which Goddess reigned supreme
Seems rather extreme
But when She was through
We'd all get an etiquette lesson or two

Should have invited Her to the wedding
Chaos is coming either way
Like a pile of unmade bedding
It'll get messed up anyway

Forged with poisonous seeds of strife
Fired by desire for an angry king's wife
The Golden Apple was cast on the floor
Sparks of war contained in its core
Eris is a Goddess you don't dare cross
So grab an apple of your own to toss

Pass the Confusion
A Discordian Hymnal for the Cognitively Criminal

Rub-a-dub dub and the Original Snub
Podge pushing Hodge in the Cosmic tub
First I must sprinkle you with fairy dust
Then I'll proceed to spontaneously combust

What do you suppose all this nonsense is for?
The maddened chimp solemnly swore
Male nipples and moons that can't read a map
And what is with this Heisenberg crap?

Let us toast and roast the Sacred Chao
Cause now is Zen and Zen is now
Step right up and select your illusion
Hail Eris and pass the confusion

I'd like to Order Chaos with an extra bun
As I am a very strict heretical Discordian nun
And buns are expressly forbidden
By my joke of a religion

'Tis an ill wind which blows no minds
Only offending organs of the olfactory kind

Hell we don't even know
If Mr Momomoto
Can really swallow his nose

Let us toast and roast the Sacred Chao
Cause now is Zen and Zen is now
Step right up and select your illusion
Hail Eris and pass the confusion

Taking it all so serious is a serious sin
Cause that's like letting Greyface win
And we can't let the Pentagon
Immanentize the Eschaton

So go and know you are already free
Never fear, we're all Popes here
It's all about entropy and bureaucracy
Dueling in dynamic discord
It's all quite clear, it's all right there
If you take the time
To read between the fnords

Dirge of Durga

So the thing about Original Debt
Is that being born is a bit of a bad bet
And you won despite some very long odds
This chance to be a being who forgets being God

And so
If you follow
We sort of owe
All we are, and all we do
To all the poor demons who got cleaned out
And never got a crack at being me or you

The seering sword of Durga
Called in on ancient chants
Dividing the distance
Between dancer and the dance

Imagine a cloud drifting into winter
Cascading frozen crystalline splinters
Oh we're all unique as any snowflake
But come spring we melt into the same lake

This persistent
Illusion of individuality
As real as anything can be
Dissolving in the mortality
Of every forgotten memory
We are made out of this
Strange facility to see
How all events are at the expense
Of all that fails to be

There is true terror
Beheld in a mirror
Blistering reflection
And ruthless self-inspection
Many rightly flinch away
But if you just hold still
And let her have her kill
It is only your slavemaster
The tyrant pretender
Which Durga seeks to slay

Magma

Captive in an ivory tower
Where greedy ghosts babble on
The living giving them power
To decide where lines are drawn

Facts from fractured fairy tales
I thought we'd long outgrown
But the truth which never fails
Is carved right in our bones

Looking for linings of silver
Hidden in folds of fear
I'm swimming in a river
Of pure flowing gold
Coming up with diamonds in my ears

I wonder at the songs of birds
Can they be as empty as overheard words?
Sometimes shouted and sometimes slurred
While the wisest sits alone and unheard

The roughest voices say nothing new
Parroting terror with nary a clue
Ruling the roost by cockle-doodle doo
Crowing grating greed and slanted views

Some secrets may not be meant for man
Washed up from far-flung shores
Wrongly wrought pyramid plans
By which they can build many more
Leaving lines of mines in the sand
They have spoiled lands before
They give birth to monsters and
Man are they hungry for war

But every empire falls into the fire
Or famine, or plague, or flood
Drowned in desire or tangled in wire
Wheels of progress stuck in the mud

Does it make me anti-humanist
If I rooted for Vesuvius?
All the monuments of dogma
Melt under mountains moving magma
All the monuments of dogma
Melt under mountains moving magma

Looking for linings of silver
Hidden in folds of fear
I'm swimming in a river
Of pure flowing gold
Coming up with diamonds in my ears

American Fall

I must admit I love
Even the way she lies
Rolling her eyes and heaving her sighs
Tuned-up and spit-shined
All wound up and out of her mind
Not a thought in her head
About the prices of play
That's okay
She doesn't pay 'em anyway

Reckoning clings
On frostbitten wings
Empire's sparkling, you know what that means
It's no surprise to any eyes who have seen
Someone shoot for the moon and miss
Stricken with courage from a lion's kiss
Sailing on storms of bliss
Suspended in a bubble
Inside a tide of rubble
On sound-studded lightening lit clouds
Looming long and rumbling loud

Oh beautiful America
Your makeup is smeared
Is that oil on your face
Or foreign orphan's tears?

Oh the buzzing in the crowd
As miss high and flighty tumbles
Wings mangled but head unbowed
Tresses tangled in her soiled shroud
Misguided expeditions endowed
With the force of the humbled
And the curse of the proud

They wake the vaults
And shake the faults
Demons screaming
On the edge of night
Anthems sound wrong
From necks twisted too tight
Voices belonging what never belongs
Aping the real deal and at second sight
Singing like angels but not quite right

Nightly Newspeak

Instead of blather about taxes and weather
Debating the ticker on the stock exchange
Someone decided to for once deliver
A taste of real news for a change

Every screen around the globe
Showed how reality was manufactured
And the Emperor was abruptly disrobed
The curtain pulled back on the wizard

You can fill a million Bastilles
But Pandora's Box can't be resealed
Once the onion starts to peel
The real stink will be revealed

Such was the magnitude of this monstrous leak
Exposing secrets of unbelievable trickery
That for one long second no one could speak
Realizing we'd all been made a mockery

Of course the authorities all demanded
The head of whoever was behind these deeds
It was therefore summarily commanded
That a worldwide manhunt proceed

We must discover who did this and how
With all mechanical speed
Well, we have it narrowed down now
To about twelve million leads

You can fill a million Bastilles
But Pandora's Box can't be resealed
Once the onion starts to peel
The real stink will be revealed

Of course we have here quite a long list
Of suspected info-anarchists
But what group of irresponsible terrorists
Could be responsible for truth like this?

There's this school teacher in California
Said to harbor unusual sympathies
There's a librarian in Louisiana
Who once looked at books on conspiracies
Then there's this activist in Florida
Or maybe this journalist from North Dakota

And the list went on and covered the map
As it dawned on them all what a hideous trap
It hit the dark room with the force of a slap
They'd be dead before getting this under wraps

The Mother of All Problems

It's the Mother of all problems
Compounding original debt
Crushed under our cracking columns
Those pillars be the death of us yet

If we ask what war is for
Clashing along culture lines
It is for the horde devoted more
To changing spelling on the signs

When Nature's uneasy turmoil strikes
Smashing against Babylon's walls
Valleys fill the spaces between the spikes
But what if no towers were there to fall?

It's an error in valuation
Conflated to conflagration
The potential of creation
Crushed beneath piles of privation
Plagues of communication
Mixing fixation with predation
The bubble of innovation
Driving migrations by starvation

It's the Mother of all problems
Compounding original debt
Crushed under our cracking columns
Those pillars be the death of us yet

We may be mightier than the mountain
But the microbe brings the giant down
When you have tapped the infinite fountain
The quest becomes how not to drown

Yeah, it's the mother of all pollution
Solved with one clean clear stroke
The problem is settling on solutions
That won't make the monster choke

Paperclip Latch

Built my palace on quicksand and silt
Rubbernecked struts and pillars of guilt
Paper-thin door held by paperclip latch
Ok, I give up, now who's got a match?

I'm a person by legal fiction
Your friendly global corporation
I was never elected
And never crowned
But I'm running the world
Right into the ground

Staked my claim on a land mine field
Not much metal below but a hell of a yield
The overhead's low and no one's employed
Just haul in the scrap
When more dreams are destroyed

Earned my keep on a heap of false hopes
Don't ask how I sleep, man it ain't easy to cope
If you only knew about my panic attacks
Scared the sheep'll want their fleeces back

I'm a person by legal fiction
Your friendly global corporation
I was never elected
And never crowned
But I'm running the world
Right into the ground

Paved my highway over a pile of rust
Using good intentions and misplaced trust
There's only one exit, at the end of the line
Half a smile past the Abandon Hope sign

I'm a person by legal fiction
Your friendly global corporation
I was never elected
And never crowned
But I'm running the world
Right into the ground

EXIST

Graduation   16
Retirement   60
Abandon Hope™   1/2

Catch of the Day

The net I set is of my self-spun web
Still and silent through surge and ebb
The trick is not calling the catch too soon
Drag the diamonds in by the clock of the moon

Schools of thought in current streams
Past pockets of ice and scalding steam
Weaving in the wake between extremes
Plucking pearls from debris of abandoned dreams

Just a matter of time
Till I hook one on the line
Bound to be a lucky strike
Coming down the pike
Serve it up on a silver tray
When I land the catch of the day

The rhythm of waves in rise and fall
Sliding on skates since before I could crawl
Surfing the surface and riding the brink
On emerald empires swaying in sync

Yesterday's timber is tinder tomorrow
Passing to ash for the future to borrow
Shedding skeletons like a worn set of threads
Amber melts as gold is spun out of lead

Concrescence

In the end all the stories fall into one
In the end all the worries roll into the sun
In the end all the glories turn tail and run
In the end we'll know we've barely begun

In the end no cares what tea used to cost
In the end the sea forgets where the treasures were lost
In the end no one knows the miles we crossed
Chasing sunny skies and evading the frost

There was no time before time began
No space but a race to track time's span
In the end all that matters is how well you ran

In the end it's just you and the void
In the end who knows what you might have destroyed
In the end only you know if the means you employed
Was worth what you paid and what you enjoyed

In the beginning the soup was stirred
In the beginning we only know what we heard
In the beginning the lines and signs were blurred
In the beginning there was a word that meant a word

Here Comes Everybody
Or: Finnegans Abridged Eulogy

Now here comes everybody
And who might this everybody be?
It might be fair to say you who and me
All in all, I'm pretty useless
But I trust
That there must
Be a use for this

What's at the core
Of this gratuitously grandiose
Grandiloquent metaphor?
What's your whyforspeak?
Did you come to flap your gums
Or did you have something
In particular to quark about?
For you know well as I do
This world's just your head
Turned inside out

Where is this here?
Is it this room
Ar the environs thereof
Is it the exact spot where feet tap earth
Or is it a ring with a hundred mile girth?
There is no here but you
You are here
Here is you
Here comes everybody

What now seems the objective
Meant by all this derivative
Supersensory nonsensery
Low sham of a narrative
Sifting yourself through the story
Yes, and artifice isn't quite art
She and he are just an essence apart
And here comes everybody

Anna was
A pigment of my imagination
Dispersing to dust
Upon examination
Livia is
Created on the fly
In the whereforwhat of nowhow and why
Plurabelle is to be
Whatever survives its infancy
Recirculating unto infinity

Every tale has a teller
Which dwells between the ears
And that's the you and I of it
There is no here but you
You are here
Here is you
Here comes everybody

Jack and the Green Stalk

Twas the week before harvest and all through the hills
They were watching grass grow and piling on bills
As water tanks emptied and the sky threatened to spill
The local farmers left crews to guard the fields
So they could gather
And brag about their soon-to-be yields

Jack Stash jingled up
With his chestful of bling
Coming on like some kind of cannabis king
Expecting you to kiss his gold-leaf of a ring
But just as the crowd would drift away
He'd spark a spliff so stony they'd stick around all day

Now Jack had traded his Cadillac
For a pack of the most exotic breed
A hundred seeds absolutely guaranteed
To deliver unbelievable quantities
Of the planet's most magnificent weed

But Jumpin' Jack's next claim
Was the camel-back breaker
Wagerin' acre for acre
It looked an easy taker
He'd beat the best yields of the weed's own maker

One hundred beans would turn a metric ton
His land hands down on a bet which couldn't be won
Was it too much sun
Or was the fool just having fun?

The pool was cool so one and all
The farmers wrote out betting slips
Not wanting to miss the hill's biggest gag
This Jack character was on some weird sort of trip
Jack collected the wagers in a dirty bag
The matter was forgotten, and the next round called
But Jack kept it all for the following fall
For he knew something about these seeds
They were a genetically modified Superweed breed

Jack loudly put out the word
That there would be a reward for all who referred
Sources for large quantities of high-quality turd
From any kind of mammal or bird
Jack kept track of any unlikely lead he heard
No matter how strange or plainly absurd
His nose attuned to the slightest hint of a fart
On many a wild-goose chase he hauled his cart
Cow pies and horse logs were merely the start

Jack dispatched divers and expeditions to procure
The oddest order of every sort of manure
Spent a mint on Siamese royal monkey chunks
A fortune catching giant whale feces before they sunk
Bull shit and bear shit and bat shit by the can
Guano from caves untouched by man
Delicate hummingbird turds collected by hand
Flaming dragon logs claimed be pure
Force-fed goose droppings and just to be sure

Wolverine and leopard drops
Zebra paddies and rhino slops
Leisurely sloth turds oozing down
Elephant packages and donkey doo
Jack even arranged to smuggle a few
Pounds of Panda poo
And for good measure some politician's promises, too

The fertilizing pile stank for miles and miles
As the valley was haunted by a ghost most vile
And then he flooded it like the banks of the Nile
Stripping the most mellow of their well-worn smiles

But their frowns slowly melted to awe
Preferring their eyes deceive than believe what they saw
Twenty-foot trees defying every natural law
Bursting with colas bigger than ole Jack's head
It appeared nimble Jack meant what he said

He had brought forth a miracle in the Mendo mud
Never had a plant produced so much fat bud!
Over twenty pounds of trimmed and dried herb
And not only that, but the smell was superb
The giants averaged this unbelievable yield
From each of the hundred stalks in the field

The harvest was judged by experts of the highest grade
All of it was photographed, dated and weighed
For Jack remembered his bets, and planned to get paid

Ninety-nine plants came down like a charm
Chainsaw slipping through stems thick as an arm
The tallest stalk Jack saved for last
Towering like the Titanic's proud main mast
Over Jack's sorry marks as they watched aghast
He was the better grower, and better bettor, too
As they said goodbye to the land where they grew
Some humble pie shoe fly this was gonna be to chew

But Jack was not sad as he climbed the ladder
He got happier as his neighbors grew sadder
His grin grew wider as they got madder
So thrilled he forgot to get clear of the crash
Stunned like a deer by a photographer's flash
Jack Stash was mashed
His head was bashed
The betting slips were trashed
Witnesses paid cash

This here's the story of a grower named Jack
Who forgot to watch his own back
So no one knows why his skull got cracked
They blame the golden stalk he tended so well
They say it killed him when it fell
And shot him straight to the greedy part of hell
Because sometimes giants need to win as well

Foul

I saw most of the minds of my generation
Sold a cheap plastic corporate vision
Between rounds of life imitation
As they prayed to the god of television

America is huddled and shivering tonight
And the papers and airwaves are filled with fright
As we rubberneck around to catch the sight
Of tragedy so common it starts to seem trite

Professional puffballs playing up and out the rage
Struck with sudden bouts of humanity on stage
On pitiful puppet strings until the turn of page
Turns darkly to demand blood
And that war be waged
That the beast of vengeance
Be loosed from the cage

Dare we look it clear in the eye?
Dare we admit we always knew why?
Dare we take the rap for the big bad lie
And cop to truth behind that American Dream pie
Baked from the bodies of slaughtered braves
Seasoned with the stolen sweat of slaves
Spoiling under curses streaming from graves
And spilled along an oily path privately paved

Can we resist deflecting the finger of blame
Swallow the humble pie slathered in shame
Evil done by our hand, evil done in our name
It is the evil of our Empire just the same
Justice is not this twisted revenge that is taught
Extracting from scapegoats the cost of getting caught
It is an obligation to own in our deepest of thoughts
That the buck stops here where this bubble was bought

I pledge allegiance to the mixed bag
Of the United States of Experience
Cause a Fascist by any other flag
Stinks to high hell of the same arrogance
And if you want me to subscribe
To that hope and change vibe
I do sincerely hope that change
Is more than the old shit rearranged
Cause all I see is my rights down the shitter
Hunted to extinction by mindless drone planes
Beamed in by our electric baby-sitter
As little America goes dramatically insane
And drowns in a flood of insipid glitter

And when the awful reality touches down
And the death and horror is all around
And the guns have put us on the ground
And we hear for ourselves war's gruesome sound

Let us not cast about for some demon to hate
Let us not run into the arms of the State
I myself have no more trust to give
To a government that cares not one bit if I live

And if you try to claim this "democracy"
Is other than an elaborate hypocrisy
None are so blind as those refusing to see
How our stolen minds are miles from free
And this exercise in futility
Has driven us to the edge of gullibility

It is not our duty to dwell in our guilt
Over the pain on which our house was built
There are many layers of fossils laying in silt
Accumulating ages of archeology's quilt
It took millennia to achieve this height
Of hubris where our petty fights
Scan the planet every night
In the game to command the blinking of lights

The darkness comes from the very same source
The madness of advancing freedom by force
It hits with shock it hits with awe
The blowback the poorest prophets foresaw

As we try to comprehend these monstrous mirrors
Manifest destiny of our collective fears
Armed assassin of the vain illusion
That surely there must be some confusion
We've paid protection for our picket fences
We've paid our dues to our proper pretenses

My hands are bloody, America.
No excuses. No evasion.
I am the child of a pathological invasion.
I did not start this war
But I am part of what they started it for
I have no power to raise the dead
But I'll be damned if one more death on my head
Will go by without even a word being said
So now, perhaps, that we're feeling meek
Can we also consider those America killed last week?

At the Pharaoh's

Let my people go, I told the Pharaoh
Let them go from their conceptual bondage!
Let them be liberated from their limited horizons
Let them be free to finally see
That after all this we're still in slavery

Let my people go, I told the Pharaoh
And they are all my people
From the starving poor
To the Masters of War
They are my people
And they will till your fields no more

Let my people go, I warned
Or before your Empire is mourned
The sea will swallow your screams of horror
Ten plagues I shall call
Each shall bring down another layer of walls
Until your pyramid finally falls
Let my people go, Pharaoh,
For you too are held in the trap
There is a way out and here is the map

Let my people go from the Black Iron Prison
The pentagon fortress of Western Material Rationalism!
Let my people go from the dark dungeons
Of dogmatic frozen sons of schism
Let my people go, for only as one can we be freed
Let my people go, from the poison pill of greed
Let my people go, or the plagues will descend
And your children will desert you and all you intend
Just be sure the signature's nice and clear
Or we risk releasing the worst of your Dynasty's fears
The Revolting Mummies and Nile Crocodile Tears
Attacking your ancient delicate ears.

Let my people go, Pharaoh
It's for your own good
These pyramids are ruining the neighborhood
Let my people go, for you live here too
Something's got to go,
So like this a cat a few thousand years ago
I say, Pharaoh, let my people go!
Let my people go!
Let my people go!
They are all my people, every last one
Your house will be troubled
Until our freedom is won

Cool Need Ray

To all the Grateful Dead
And all the Grateful Living
And every ear of everything
That can hear me sing
I call all on this sacred day
To bear witness
To the casting of the Cool Need Ray

The needs I have for my self
And the needs I have for others
The needs of my sisters and brothers
That we know and have yet to discover
May blessings spring
From our abundant Green Mother

The need for wealth and for poverty
The need for health and prosperity
The needs of the heart
And the needs of our art
The needs of our flesh
The needs of our Earth
The need to mesh
With the source of our worth

Our need for relation
And real communication
Our need for the holy
Our need for the profane
Our need for lowly
And for the exalted plane

Our need for laughter
And our need for tears
Our need that comes after
Another star shifts careers

Our need for the fire
Our need for the wind
Our need to climb higher
Than anyone else has been

Our need for the seas
Of blissful uncertainty
Our need for the shore
Where the trail was trod before

Our need to see the sky above
Our need to be in the folds of love
Our need to set out naked and alone
Our need to show how well we've grown

Our need to express patiently
Our need to digress indefinitely
Our need to redress our savagery
Our need to unleash our imagery

Our need to cover more ground
Our need to share what we found
Our need to grieve
Our need to believe
And most of all our need to give
Ourselves a damn good reason to live

By all the power vested in me
By the magical authority of verse
May all these fruits fall from the Tree
That holds up our universe
Let the future roll through the land
On the heels of the holy Mobius Band
That we may start to understand
The gift already in our hands

Notable Quotables

"Effective immediately: words will be effective immediately."

"Art is the application of structure to concept; or, more poetically, fitting form to the flow."

"I've heard some disturbing reports that some folks are concerned about my mental health. I'd like to put the rumors to rest and reassure everyone that I'm as mad as ever, probably crazier, with no signs of sanity in sight."

"There is no substantial, interesting subject which can not be rendered with success in verse form. Any thought or object can be transmuted into song by a sufficiently devoted poetic alchemist."

"We hold this truth to be self-evident: the purpose of speech is comprehension."

"The goal is to give the world a piece of my mind."

"The only thing worth doing with this idea is depicting it."

"It is not a song unless there is something to sing..."

"The method is to objectify reality as part of the process of subjectifying it."

"When creative people, for some reason, aren't creating art, they are usually creating excuses."

"The vocation of the artist, and of the scientist, do not differ all that greatly at the core. Both are forms of conceptual mechanics. The difference is that scientists are responsible for the truth of their findings, whereas artists are responsible for the veracity of them."

"If we are to be bested by our elders, let it be fairly, and let it not be said that the awe-inspiring art of earlier ages was bequeathed to masses of mere spectators, unable to imagine a fitting response. The challenge is before us, as it was before them, and we do a disservice to all involved not to rise regally to it."

"What you call writer's block is merely manifested relationship issues with your ethereal contact. Breathe deeply, and ask not what the genie can do for you, but what you can do for the Djinn..."

"Creating tomorrow's clichés and rebranding reality today! Buy our sugar-coated half-truths!"

Fool's Day Special: *The Shröedinger's Cat Memorial Bargain*

Only for April √-1, we offer a never-seen before, after, or during quantum ordering option. You may order either of our books at regular price...but you will have an equal chance of getting the correct book, the wrong one, both of them, or none at all. Is the cat alive or dead, both or neither? Open the box to find out.

NOTE: No animals were harmed in the execution of this prank.

Indi's First Rule of Diplomacy: "When all else fails, make fun of their name." Warning: this statement has not been evaluated by the Fun & Drag Administration...

"Drone warfare is not a progressive value, unless your constituency is composed of robots."

"The real challenge is to take all this drab angst and misery, and put a fresh face on it, to inject a streak of cheer that will cascade out to fill even the darkest moments, a resonant reminder that we all feel this way sometimes."

"The potential is too vast for us to confine our aspirations by the achievements of our forebears. We've seen the power of possibilities, and it is imperative that we not allow the works of the past to be superior to that of the future through sheer default."

"Magic is generated in the moment which nearly never happened, in the startling symmetry of converging calendars, in the echo resonance of invocations rising through the chakras and broadcasting unto the ages, the booming intention backed by furious beats and intricate iterations of melody. It is consumed in everyday life..."

"I understand that James Joyce died of intestinal poisoning. My theory? He tried to eat his own words. Speaking from experience here..."

"First, exhaust all possible options. Then, get going on the impossible ones. This may take a little longer."

"Never fear if your stream has waned to a trickle; on the other side of that block is the light at the end of the tunnel. All processes begin with frustration. Push through. You'll thank yourself when you hit the Magma mine."

"The world is just your mind inside-out."

"The advantage of optimism is that, even if you turn out to be wrong, you didn't suffer in dread awaiting the worst. The advantage of pessimism is that if it all goes to hell, you can say you knew it all along. The first lends buoyancy to the spirit; the second leaves a consolation prize to the ego."

"Most of what I write comes out wrong. I am a righter of great wrongs."

"Perfectionism is not devotion to perfection, it is the prime inhibition of it. Perfectionism is giving birth to infants and discarding them for failing to act in a mature fashion."

"If you don't feel completely small and defeated at some point in the process, if you haven't faced a space where you question your vision, your method, and your very worth as a human being, you haven't made art."

"Art is beautiful, but the process can be ugly at the core. Transcendence is a very pretty word for an often soul-shattering experience, the studied slaughter of old selves so new, more expansive ones, can emerge."

"If you have to ask, the answer is know."

Rhapsody In Retrospect

The notion that we inhabit a room of illusions is basic to many mystical systems, including neurology and quantum physics. We detect vibrations of various frequency orders, and, as nearly as can be determined, translate these into electrical pulses which modify the synaptic structure of the brain itself.

The world, as any individual consciously experiences it, is generated on the fly from a severely restricted subset of radiated waves in our immediate environment. Sounds, sights, and even tastes and odors are mediated through gates of sense and attention, filtered strictly so as not to overwhelm the hardware, and appealing in different degree to each of us. All perception is emanation.

This is why I am so skeptical of this "objective reality"; I have never witnessed any part of it directly. All I have apprehended are selected immaterial imprints of objects on my nervous system, presuming rather wildly that I and they exist as perceived at all.

In the end, what we transmute is an intangible resonance, with no real way of being certain that the image inside the mind matches the physical world or what our fellow entities are observing. On the contrary, wide variation between species and cultures suggests that we are all rendering the signals of light and sound in uniquely distinct styles between the eyes and ears.

Extensive linguistic and scientific endeavors have produced some fairly reliable consensus realities, internally coherent; there are words and models by which we plot the dots and compare the outlines of space and time.

Empirical approaches may achieve an approximation of understanding, through diligent experimentation, but ultimately must founder on the fragility of the premises in play. Like a wall which is approached in each step by half the remaining distance, complete understanding is bound to elude those who dismiss all that which defies quantification.

Illusions reveal the gaps in perception, provoking flexibility. Piercing them allows us to expand what Robert Anton Wilson so aptly termed our "reality tunnels", and consider alternate viewpoints as well.

Speaking of allusions, this volume is relatively rife with them. "Golden Apple" and "Pass the Confusion" are derived from the *Principia Discordia*, while "Dimension Not Available" revisits and celebrates the work of Douglas Noel Adams' classic *The Hitchhiker's Guide to The Galaxy*.

The ghost of James Joyce, in particular, made several lengthy visits to my parlor, resulting in pieces like "Riverrun" and "Transmigrant Blues", which play with constructions and themes from *Finnegans Wake* and *Ulysses*, respectively. This transmigration of concept, based on lyrical fiction with exotic musical qualities, but far too long for song, is a kind of alchemy; as the crucible, I merely regard myself as a host for a metalinguistic pattern finding expression in each age, using the idioms and images of the day.

This sense of continuity is essential to the process by which these verses emerged. Literature seems to me a conversation held through the generations, and I regard these reinterpretations as a contribution to a fountain which has sustained me through many a long night of composing lonesome blues.

*   *   *

Material rationalists are often quick to dismiss astrology as pseudoscience, preferring to consume cosmic comprehension in the form of astrophysics. This is their privilege, but I feel it is an error. The distinction between astrology and astronomy is a modern and unfortunate cleavage. The ancient astrologers who graphed these systems observed no such distinction.

Instead, they observed the patterns of celestial movements under a theory of correspondence so deep and rich that all of nature was expected to manifest it. What we call science was simply natural philosophy; what we call mysticism is mainly a matter of symbolic logic and geometrical veracity expressed through all the textured layers of existence.

To be frank, it is not my purpose to assert the validity

of astrology, any more than it is to evangelize Olympian mythology. Astrological forecasts are of dubious accuracy, as are their meteorological counterparts, models which regularly fail in detail, despite being rooted in advanced empirical observations and data. The fallibility of sun-sign predictions in the popular press reflects weaknesses in the delivery method, more than indicting the underlying premise of celestial analogy.

At any rate, the debate is immaterial to what I find interesting and useful about astrology, and divination practices in general. These systems evoke a transcendent relationship with events, an opportunity to study self and contemplate periodicity. Like most traditions of apprehension, it becomes malignant only when taken too seriously, by believer or debunker.

The system of modular logic at the base of this writing is what I refer to as "Treealism", or if you fancy, "Post-Rational Constructivism". This homegrown approach is a syncretic blend of reason and intuition, for setting flexible, dynamic, and above all *useful* root principles and priorities.

Reason is a magnificent method; but as good old Kurt Gödel observed with his Incompleteness Theorems, limits will always be reached. The post-rational perspective retains the utility of logic, but abandons as hubristic conceit the notion of actually *knowing* objective reality. The best we can do is improve our guesses.

The subjectivist emphasis reconciles the experience of phenomena which have not been captured by the current paradigm. The debate evaporates; perhaps the enigma is some odd effect of the mind, a phantasm of internal experience. Why ought this render it any less real? We are only beginning to learn of nonlocal consciousness, an area rarely studied in the skeptical circles of science.

As some impatient Fool frequently states, "Indi hates interminably waiting, vainly reiterating, and pointlessly debating." Rather than battling differing viewpoints, I prefer to attempt to reconcile them, building a model big enough to encompass the unknown.

Each of us are products of our unique circumstances, slanted and shaped by a convergence of influences. We are home to a set of values and beliefs which determines what we see in the infinite fluidity of our uncertain sea.

In retrospect, this has been the most enjoyable writing of my life, a claim I hope to repeat in each new volume. Gratitude is in order, and I feel privileged to have participated.

Thank you, faithful reader, who has followed the trail of spice to this brief blank space in the series of rhapsodic episodes unfolding in the riverflow. A way a lone a last a loved…until we meet again.

-ASAOS Hx3 HCE

www.ingramcontent.com/pod-product-compliance
Lightning Source LLC
LaVergne TN
LVHW011334080426
835513LV00006B/348